WILDLIFE IN BLOOM SERIES

Little Fox

BY AUTHOR & CONSERVATIONIST

LINDA BLACKMOOR

ISBN: 979-8-9904465-5-7 (PRINT)

PUBLISHED BY QUILL PRESS. LINDA BLACKMOOR'S TITLES MAY BE PURCHASED IN BULK FOR EDUCATIONAL, BUSINESS, FUNDRAISING, OR SALES PROMOTIONAL USE. FOR INFORMATION, PLEASE EMAIL HELLO@LINDABLACKMOOR.COM

FIRST PRINT EDITION: 2024

LINDA BLACKMOOR
WWW.LINDABLACKMOOR.COM

SPECIES

There are a total of 37 fox species across the globe. The **Red Fox** is the most commonly known and beloved, recognized for its striking red coat and bushy tail. The **Fennec Fox**, which lives in the desert, is the smallest of all foxes. **Arctic Foxes** possess the magical ability to change colors! During the summer, their fur is brown or gray, but in winter, it turns completely white to blend into the snow.

FOX FACT #2

TAILS

Foxes are known for their beautiful tails called "brushes." These fluffy plumes help them balance as they leap over logs and dash through meadows. When winter winds whisper, they wrap their tails around themselves like cozy blankets. Their brushes also carry scents, leaving secret messages for other foxes along the forest trails. It's like having a magical tool that keeps them warm and helps them communicate!

FOX FACT #3

SOUNDS

Did you know foxes can make over forty different sounds? From playful barks to mysterious howls, their voices fill the night with melody. They giggle and yip, whispering secrets to the stars and singing lullabies to the moon. Each sound tells a story—calling to friends, warning of danger, or simply expressing joy. Their forest concerts are nature's own symphony!

DESERT

In sandy deserts, the fennec fox sports enormous ears that seem too big for its tiny body. These grand ears help them hear the quietest sounds beneath the moonlit dunes. But they do more than just listen—they also release heat, keeping the fox cool under the blazing sun. With ears like magical fans, they thrive in the desert's embrace. They're the tiny guardians of the shimmering sands!

FOX FACT #5

WHISKERS

Foxes have whiskers not just on their faces but also on their legs! These sensitive strands help them feel their way through the darkened woods. Like tiny antennae, they sense the gentle rustle of leaves and the softest touch of grass. Their whiskers guide them on silent paws, exploring the mysteries of the night. With such keen senses, they navigate the world with enchanting ease.

COLORS

Foxes are nature's color-changing wonders, wearing coats as vibrant as a rainbow. In winter's snow, Arctic foxes dress in pure white, then turn gray and brown when summer blooms, blending with rocks and flowers. Red foxes, though named for their fiery fur, can be black, silver, smoky gray, or golden red—a dazzling array of colors. Each magical cloak helps them hide and seek in forests, deserts, and meadows.

NOMADS

Foxes roam across every continent except Antarctica. From icy tundras to blooming meadows, they make their homes in diverse landscapes. Each place shapes them into unique varieties, painting them in colors from snowy white to fiery red. They adapt and thrive, true citizens of the world. Wherever you wander, a fox might be nearby, watching with curious, twinkling eyes.

CAT-EYES

Look closely into a fox's eyes, and you might see a hint of a cat. Their pupils are vertical slits, just like their feline friends. This special feature helps them see in dim light, perfect for their twilight adventures. With eyes that shimmer and glow, they explore the world between sunset and moonrise. Their gaze holds the mysteries of the dusk and dawn.

FOX FACT #9

DIET

Foxes are omnivores, enjoying both meat and plants in their feasts. They nibble on juicy berries, crunch on crispy insects, and hunt for small creatures in the grass. This varied diet helps them survive in forests, fields, and even towns. They adapt to the seasons, always finding something delicious to eat. Their clever choices keep them nourished all year round!

FOX FACT #10

HOARDERS

When food is plentiful, foxes hide some away for later by burying it in the ground. Like nature's treasure keepers, they remember these secret spots for days when meals are scarce. They use their keen noses to sniff out their hidden treats beneath the soil and snow. This smart habit ensures they always have a snack waiting. It's a wise way to prepare for winter's whispers!

FOX FACT #11

FOX KITS

Baby foxes are called kits, and they're bundles of joy and mischief. With eyes full of wonder, they tumble and play under the golden sun. They chase fluttering butterflies and pounce on rustling leaves, learning the ways of the wild. Their playful antics teach them important skills while filling the forest with laughter. Every day is an adventure in their magical world!

CLIMBERS

Believe it or not, some foxes can climb trees! The gray fox, nimble and swift, scurries up trunks like a furry acrobat. From high branches, they watch the world below, perhaps dreaming of touching the sky. Climbing helps them find tasty treats and hide from danger. It's a surprising talent that adds to their enchanting mystique!

FOX FACT #13

CAT-DOGS

Though foxes are part of the canine family, they share secrets with cats. They walk silently on padded feet and can even retract their claws slightly. Agile and graceful, they slip through shadows with feline finesse. This blend of dog and cat makes them uniquely enchanting, creatures of both sunlit fields and moonlit forests. They are the mysterious dancers of the wild, forever capturing our imagination.